**sybil
unrest**

sybil
unrest

Larissa Lai & Rita Wong

VANCOUVER | NEW STAR BOOKS | 2013

NEW STAR BOOKS LTD.
107 — 3477 Commercial Street
Vancouver, BC V5N 4E8   CANADA

1517 — 1574 Gulf Road
Point Roberts, WA 98281   USA

www.NewStarBooks.com
info@NewStarBooks.com

New Star Books acknowledges the financial support for our publishing program from the Canada Council for the Arts; the Government of Canada through the Canada Book Fund; and the Province of British Columbia through the British Columbia Arts Council and the Book Publishing Tax Credit.

Cataloguing information for this book is available from Library and Archives Canada, www.collectionscanada.gc.ca.

Cover design by Oliver McPartlin
Cover image: M. Connor
Printed on 100% post-consumer recycled paper
Printed and bound in Canada by Gauvin Press
First printing, September 2013

shrinkwrapped pushy
condemns on sale
dill pickle harmless
let her strap on
law's garters
lend me your tears
cunt remand
loved fist
loose brigand
safe sects
nimble clamps
over and over
just a mother
hole in the wall
tribade's revelations
wet pinch of salt
on the stroke of midknife

fish wife mothers pearl
mistress masters secret sex
nun plus nun is none
the sun in her hair
down below her knees
where it's safe
slipshod
the heel may gape
but the shoes last forever
and ever amen

manned by the world bunk
those 3-piece suited heels gash
& smother earth
skyscrapers spent, flaccid
i m f---'d
the bleak small inherit the dearth
none left
butt the roaches
global swarming encroaches

couched in no uncertain germs
warfare's new upholstery
the empire's new caves
cache nuclear arms
the right always finds what it left
the part never completes the hole
under investigation
overdetermined and overseen
seer sucker
the unstitched garment puckers
the subaltern cannot peek

her futures gambled on the casino market
stuck in the loop o
stealth martins, lockheed dupes
bombard e-bay
trickle down eco anomie
bears and curses
bulls and purses
blink an i
swerve on the roadmap
too destruction
sadomarketism

to buy a fine pig
can't feel a fling
nerves want a happy ending
organism organizes
orgasmic orangutangs
dreamt the experiment was just a dream
dreamt i was a butterfly drowned in butter
dreamt i was man
codes switched
helix froze over
i dream of genes
irregular manifestation
prehensile where before the bone stopped
pheremone memory
tenticular anemone
waving waving
hello god good garden gap

mechanical subway miss
intones please mind the gap
regular intervowels
special administrative lesion
bird markets flew
over the google mast
mushed and bushed
trampled by the swoosh
in corporate predictability
iconomic bust
shush pending on
the leap from
liberal to liberation

leap hog factory farm
industrial replication
love's lepers lost
mimicry introduces mutation
charmed I'm sure
autocorrect capitalizes the subject
the pig pisses next to the pig pissing next to the pig
passing the cellular difference
stalled on the hill
clutching the genome's
correction mutation
in time with the tao
of the piglet disney bought
of the plight that jack built
of the p-p-p prevention
prison pride revision
the application of autoimmune
impertinences imperative to the imp
limp limping of lipase conversion
the religo-military-capital
expensive intensive leaving and getting
the branding of the pig
peeing and pooing
oohing and ahhing over the fat
slice lean meat
in neat plastic packages

girls chant to the pigs:
no justice, no donuts!
corporate mounties hail mary
batons erect, spray pepper
choke on their stiff collars
hey gay marriage
the repressed all enraged
petty mores disgorged
red and black mice trounce & tramp
entire cities engineered
from celebration into situationist
tunnels in the edifice
stubborn rodents
gnaw neigh keuih day
mind the pap
all bull
say the old boys in gowns
noise in town:
enough homoerratic foreflay
strip your uniform
now boys
let's see your
inner who man

few men chew
chew choose the train
whether they built the tracks
or drove the last spike
or bought the containers
that make up the train
that goes on the tracks
that make up the railway that cn built
that took over grand trunk pacific
that absorbed central vermont
that swallowed hudson's bay
that acquired newfound line
that inaugurated super continental
that monked a hump yard
that leased aircraft turbo trains
that derailed to via
that ran to the crown
that merged with cp
that got into telecom
that restructured again
that sold its hotels
that loosed its caboose
that privatized profits
that bought illinois central
that received wisconsin
that grabbed great lakes too
that nabbed bc rail
that took elgin, joliet & eastern
before amtrak and fairmont
could slug to its mother
and go under cover
no point reinventing the deal
that worked so well the first time
this little piggy loves the free market economy
in the guise of democracy
cries we we we
all the way to the bank

see the crazy fox ju!mp
over trickledown falsies
graze through
gross distorted product
nestled into
formula franchises
dogged pursuit
through boring malls
tracks sidewalk cracks
for non-cents sniff
whiff that green
bed of roysters
knows, nudges
diurnal libration
tidalectics flow
earth's rubric
truces & seduces

trounces and bounces
fabric cubed
prophets escalate as the coloured
squares tune
earth's meek inheritance
outer spatial vibrations
inner temple visions
sip but don't inhale
hey my buddy buddha hey man
ray gun
barbarella tumble fleeced and feathered
pickets were pocked anyway
bought by spock babies
formula fed and spewing algorithms
we wave our fronds
and ascend the stareway
safe in our purchases and pins

winnows from
central dogma
ruminants
happy as a stammer
or urban planners'
wham, bam
tensile mam
holler and collar
stock exchange shams
if the shares are all blown
her hoards on estrange
detourne and enthrall
resume and recall
the listening wind

to hold what the ship cannot
wayward cargo trips the wind
wakes the unfed
wet trail back to shore of origin
more than bodies arrive
more than work transpires
invoke the claw
perfect the pretext's
protective rhetoric
say "safe" mean "unclean"
we applaud the walls
beg blindness from bodies that confirm complicity
elicit the difference
deter the innocent
refer the ambiguous ambulant amphibian
illegal until proven guilty
want the labour without the body
surplus halo
nervous nimble nexus
old slice
temporal doom
pirates of penance
blips ahoy
screen shudders as grid hiccups
corridor collapsing
current passé
seeks sweet vacuum courant
the shock of recognition was overwhelming

televised revulsion
armed patrols
against anadromous androgynes
pixellated shot at black hair
signals amber, red light
distract the gaze
from canada's expert destruction corporation
littoral spectators
witless repeat-rich history
repelled, rusted, repressed
undertow: rudderless economy
bodies adrift
flail against smug myopia
continental shrift

utopia by distraction
interaction scripted
relief without prevention
continuous content confessional denominator:
i slept with my lycanthropic boyfriend's teenage feral son
in a high security nuclear facility
while high on crystal meth
accompanied by a sixteen piece brass band
in hopes of winning a million dollars
while other contestents waited in a sweatshop in shenzhen
decorated with apsaras and buddha heads
agon of capital
mechanical repetition + survival wages
big brother's other sister
yours was the weakest wink

drink the vision
watch the scream
dream the snuff
congratulate the contradiction
we couldn't have done it without you

quotidian terror
knifed and niked
our backs
tromped and stumped
stunned by spectacle farce
realty teeters
middlefingers
dystopia by subtraction
marked economy
stabs false prices
onto water, air, land
stuck pig grunts
pumped full of antibiotics
psychotic bacon
beckons
know thy enzyme
transgenic estrogenic
effluvium transfers
into your porcine gut
glow-in-the-dark hashbrowns
come with the order
spudmuffin
let's haunch

grow in the park hallucinations
corn born corn
the colonel's boys lick and sniff
stiff coiffed southern fresh
off the flight
the border's horders
in starched shirts
unicyle the re-
interpretation of travel documented
to suit the spiffy
while cirrus clowns
intone
give the dog a bone
old man laughs up his sleeve
fishes for the kernel
of ruth and her book flaps open
in the same place that you die
i will die
we travel
over and over
it's just another holy roller

charged happenstance
in the wake of
tidal genocide :
thousands of turtles roll over in
that mass grave, the oceanic bedslide
trawled and mauled
oh palimpsest of crushed shells
succour a queer sorrow
unappeasable and viral
vestiges of heads that will not
erupt through hallowed skin
into dizzying love
swim in the wake of your death,
my death, our deaths, soaked
in cumulus disturbance
long for electric release
but pent in transnational circuits
await more deaths
as capital's corpses accumulate

housed on rooftops
feet fete without earth
spirit of the weak
raised poolside
fifteen famous porn stars stimulate
economy
abstraction escalates
cash as concept
waxes material
corporate cops regulate muscular flows
tear perforated strip
to detach soul at point of entry
nation's heart triple bypassed
tremblequivers
senses nervous surge of global power
brokers shudder
as social organism flips right out
alternate current gushes to haunted gap
now you see it
now you don't

robocrop distrot
slimed and stymied
port of sentry
incriminate testosterone gentry
disgruntle suburban complacency
crumpled crestfallen
falacious fellatio
primetime news
redundant moneyspeak
derivative divergence
divulging dischord
demonic harmonic
of the cocacola commercial
tinny addictions
mass collusions collapse
denuded

lesser collisions slide sideways
overpass grows over
moss lichen prairie grass
tomatoes on vine
in big sun
in hot rain
the lyric panegyric returns
glorious mutation
the same but
gorgeous gorgon different
all tongue and lip
and hair and there
outrides dogged apocalypse
follows wet night
twist twining
slip gliding
into the cricked cracks the hallowed hollows
left after the last flesh has rotted and returned
to earth
i'll glow if i have to
adapt the toxin
adopt the biological discontinuity
adore the exhausted
embrace the uranium depleted
loving the alienated
purity skids on pink lake
birds rock
to their own conference
after the fire

has been put out with gasoline
pyres flare
tempers flail
flames lick underbelly's slick bulge
slinging love like there's no tomorrow
sweaty thrush
grip and crawl
through urban sprawl
hunger growls
hirsute and rehearsed
mining persistent thrall
a dim sweetness
somehow

moment melts
but packaging's half-life
deteriorates millenia
time after crime
our hour's glass
over salt and sand
compulsive returns
bacterial and subatomic fascination
we count hairsplitting headaches
as massive machines profess
universality whole
galaxies spill stars and dirt
while uniforms stripe over
all the crises of arabia
hear 'here'
we adored the veils and fireworks
of our own making
wiped our bloodwet fists
on shirtbacks greenbacks
pretended not to see
biochemical clocks
tick off crocodile
tears weep themselves
as sweet sister dried-eyed collects
flesh of her flesh
off history's concrete
and we won't say who's responsible

& who's wounded in reaction
melancholy electron to erection
pectoral to electoral, a schwarzeneggerian flex
feral grin all teeth and no trust
no god no american fist no american thrust no thank you
no tea party no salada commercial either
no monarchy malarky
eagle as indigenous not as uncle slam
uncle slime stinky climb on the backs of whose turtle island

sexual devolution
prime mate ate prime rib
adam keeps the quick pick extra
o bone of my bone
greed cancerous & terminal
harrows marrow of biologically determined
we worship intel inside o beloved
proteus of inedible protein sequencing
mechanical magnetism
aids usb connection
renders serial port obsolete
i mourn the wire
while long distance feeling
discovers satellite coverage
deepen my dish baby
i'll go digital
my boston will marry
your tea party for $9.95/mo.
plus a one-time installation fee

call 1-900-lone-dog
for psychic mistress while
salt-fisted girls
in margaritavilla
pack
distressed meat
on disgruntled bones
unsavoury conundrums
thrum
in their harnesses
waiting for the buckle to loosen
its red imprint
to fade from
carnal evidence
retreat into ruddy sweat production
when all else pales

escape this agent's
communal miss-tery render
hysterical truth for the record
meat is sweeter salted
my cordial leer
directs different traffic
east meets eden
race under pressure
grace made to measure
gender's fender bends the trace
leans into wind
charms esoteric set
to table pining pieces
before moratorium imposes
"in cod we trust"
i joy my fake id
prosthetic aesthetic
sighs borg no longer
technotreasure outperforms
all other vehicles of its class

lumpen bored with
wage slavery
muscles into
historical tendons
flex consensual
plummet
as flaming moths
negotiate
fiery deaths
distress was her middle name
as she damselled the barely dented machine's
sticky black cogs
a nipple caught
in the gears of longing
luster lucre
oiled cognition
televised villages
spectral peers

machines R us
our cables couple on sexed insertions
aliens invaded ages ago
we adore their rapid rate
thru veins
brain this love story
intimate hybridity
we gorge on microchips
bioengineer the salsa
cha cha cha to the twelve step
recovery of our collective
cyborg consciousness
resist the transistor
sister or let radio waves
flag your heart down
information highway thrills speed
charms chambers to virtual tryst
surrender to the vibes man
"amor vincit omnia"
wink wicked wives
all fishy and artificial
scale and tale
boast in the machine
(maw agape)
original fleshpot dictionary
already doing double duty

two signs of the coin
between your legs
a manyhearted joy
of no return
harbours
heron's lovely cry
bittermelon belly
o regenerate
starfishlike
earthen auricle
mown down
broods lobe
sprouts stubborn
shimmers tertiary eyes
why open?

men's lens lends
overload of intimate information
sets will to chill
on buddha's beautiful ears
open to the om
eye's third watch
blinks peace through rigorous training
orange robe your independence
praise the madonna
don't go for second best baby
octopus the bulbous
ahead of suction cupping
tentiticular guarantees only tense tents
testing empty lots
soup hope yes
solidarity yes
but longing on-line
vancouver's wet season
damps laundry to replication
of spores and mould

s&m:
sorrow mulled
over autumnal fire
leaves
a spiked mystery
in my chest
sidereal mace
sullenly mothering
shadowy hungers
mewl while
silent movies'
shuddermoments
merge with the urge
to suckle
murmurous convergence

murderous resurgence
golems of oligopoly gather grammar
old empire's well-trained subjects
hood predicate's ironic reversals
communicate better in their english
than they do
dangle participles
poor construction
last century's logic said
we'd never learn
ghost our bodies through
proper pronunciation slips distance
racialized lunge for glottal stops
exchange intimate vernaculars
choice body and body only or
language and language only
quick fix labour's assembly line
we rome our roads leading
cuff our twin cubs
as empire rebirths
"same diff"
against lyncanthropic throbbing
bulge of canine eye
the better to see you
sharp press of teeth against own lips

packing mackerel
like there's no tomorrow
angry modifiers
do institutional calisthenics
door guardians gnawed off
paw on the ball
paw on the baby
sad stone, sad stone
an uneven pear
pings

pear seeds what peach stones
goat scaped by global flows
our ethno financed
by deflated federalism
we mark our doors
girl gorillas blood bandanas
hope vengeance
will pass us over
we engine our numbers
miss cloud nine
by hare's breath
stuck in ten's tepid tent
moon rabbits its multiplication
table topic for tennis
fast paddle over white net
our river teams
against current
pong of birth and fishrot

glossy crotchshot
in a hongkong subway
sells jeans
sheen of commerce
commences, imparts
we ching ruins or
evangelical bankers
strewn across the skyline
like so many neon signs
arched breath unzips
her marketed anatomy
this labyrinth town, its focal glow
astounds

beast within is best
in enemy arms
or canary's coal mine
tarred and feathered
by the same boss
girl our goodness
while ewes bleat refusal
we jack the cracker
fm radios the past
post-punked in new romantic
bombs our harlequin fingers nimble threads
camels eye the needle
as we eye heaven
on the other side of complicity
capital beckons sweet
as freedom in a tight skirt
violence loves desire
as meat loves leer
mammon's mama-san moves mountains
holy shock thin veil
for fascination
agape quells what wells
cri de cur of nervous organism
hankering after rich man's bone

hack   hawk   haul ass
where past
wear pants
the posture of packing
cracked patriarchy
shuffled deck dick duck
yes duck the shit
and no i'm not
happy to see you
when my civic dissonance
proclaims an
upstanding citizen

hk skyline bands
consumers' electronic
to hawkers wash 'n' wear
and do run run
from the rickshaw man
with the golden gun
we bond our babes
in lewd 'n' loose
goose as in mother
rhymes for crying out loud
not again grime the plates
tectonic while the dish
runs away with the loon

ragged to rigid
goosed and slandered
trick of downed ren min bi
rich men's bones
turned real maternal butch

so hold me mom
in your long arms

law's longing for nuclear
capability cash and carry
our states of rogue solidity
can't gas without chamber
even at town pump
our exxon slicks
foul howl of birdcall
catcall wolf whistles
poxx in a boxx
deoxyrided down the cellular escalator

sod in episode
slips lip to dry land
we water our light
rapid transactions
in dialectics dim twin beams
deer caught in crossfire
agony of calgary
oil crooks on all sides
bleed bleat or leap
from dow chemical to alchemical
from alcan to ali baba
petro can but mobil can't ice
what rises falls as dew
forty thieves or forty nights
desert's emptiness is treasure
capital can't cap

gestures towards absence
allure of failure fills
heart's almost stopped watch
ticks countdown to
yesterday's launch
picnic all the theatres
of all our wars
sized small medium
culprit at large in
hope's extra vacuum
we wash our hands
antiseptic wringing
unaware toxin's already
entered bloodstream
doting aunties birth
what can't be borne
clipped wings contemplate
hollow bones regrowth
say 'aye' to re-subject
all in favour

"i" resurrect "oui"
because the heart
won't stop
tackling
how plenitude
could shatter habit
how germinate
could smash
inhospitable lurch
to failed utopias

i-topia books our digital
revolutions six weeks in advance
slick surface informs
highways mapped on wireless connection
i'm fido
mobility's dear faith
love me
love my cog

ignition flickers contagious contiguous
sex weakens diatribe
that's why
defiant vulvas venture
through patriarchal corridors
their ragged magma
turns convention to convection
from diode to subduction zone
girlfriend might moan
for the long night's
crone performs
catholic money slandering
tricks in lieu of
subservience

weekly menu feeds babely
tribe our beloved amazon
gushes effusive
i'm lovin' it
explaining her beef
as die cast
on probability of profitability
we clock our overdraft
in times new roman
loose mysteries
twist forked laughter
as goddesses sign in triplicate
'the pleasures of being multiple'

hailed wonder of being several:
while she goes on dispensing
business-as-usual
another she sits
in silent mourning
another she
actively seeks distraction
but the barbed dolls
stiff with artifice
leak plastic trauma
choke on
missing addresses

rendered inoperative by viral horses
our trojan interface seeks
indiscriminate revenge against those who sleep
on-line regardless of dreams
my distracted double
dolls herself up
sweetened by sham
our vulnerable firewalls bird ashes
to rise as electronic copy
do you read me?
emotion registers
cash on the nail
sorrow sells charity to 1-800
irritation buys convenient packages
anger markets management to white collars while
laughter irons redux in fresh paint
retro palettes and en route magazine declares
the death of cool

going through the notions
economists pantomime
the pollution of oceans
the razing of old growth
on spreadsheets
foolish eyes burn, water,
no safe specs
under the drum of the monitor
unreliable hoards
no protection against
the bellicose lair of the bush

burning as though
accusation is evidence
innocent until proven filthy
by supremacy's medieval darkening
cruise sadistic missiles
in airspace internationalized
on prime time tv
set clocks to progress
as capital backpeddles
tainted goods
low dose over the counter
intelligence on high alert
reason sold as empty addiction
to barren media
barrelling dollars per
down the barrel of a pun

parallax means
we both sight the bullet
but don't know who
will be struck dumb
by the dump truck
of progress
except extinction
rebounds on its makers
so we attempt to swerve from
fatal to natal, seek mère, metonymy
hope for graceful anatomy,
a womb with a view, passage
for coming generations

paradox of measurement
stretch body's changes over
geological clocks astronomical distance
we politic our firm hands certainty
rage against the bad dream
in time's other pocket
find navigational instruments
we loved once
before the killings
in sea time
when the root was there
without the fascist impulse
something shimmers in the palm

pearl lodged in grievous silt
burnt embrace, survivors' guilt
knowledge shrivels bitter without action
though we can't measure what is enough
striving pulls in tension to love's undertow
raise courtyards and cathedrals
to the f-word, freedom-bound
sexing the charred remains
of human effort, resuscitate
old earth knowledges or die trying

cycle do around still
live and leave death
to those who mete it best
guilt spills grief in torrential circles
all the world's a page
out of paradigms box ← pandoras box
we militarize noxious spites
on fundamental fury
remember panda's mischief
hope on a hotrod
promises babylon's babies
faith to fate is not a requirement of this degree

why the change?

virago will do
    to delay lethe
  to chant political showdowns
  mettle outgrows backpedal
is same a revolutionary straitjacket?
  reinventing will, "consequential disobedience"
    granting institutions the third degree,
  try sector, trimester, perpetual scrutiny,
slowly bound with china
    adopt garment labour
    filament lesbos to
polyglot postwhore girls

female warrior, bad tempered

greek ref.
oblivion/forgetfulness

pre-war innocence
           envelopes my greensleeve
liturgic him travails new world's
old wires
    wife my slim fish
wet slips
a pocket full of poesy
we plague our chicken flu
           asian as avian
invasions bloody
           evasian
punish poultry celled mutant
           in cages of pragmatism's invention
a tissue a tissue
    we all fall
           for the dollar
you are
my singapore girl
           a great way to pry

[handwritten annotations: "public religions worship", "painful", "connection to earlier poem", "poetry"]

63

not open for business
unless your little bird cunt says so
    heartened glass glances
    feracious green lungs
        igneous love
        chars this pair of palms
        charged heart glows
        turns teller machines into fenetrum
            separation into reparation
trust delivers

trading on insider knowledge
    blond shades industrial strength
        our average child
chooses fair or feral   teeth sharp
as families feud our pilgrim's modest touch
    motive charged on american
while orient leaves home without
our engines manifest destiny
    formalae express zero sum as second best

legalized, eagle-eyed gambling
fails, flails
a shock market convulses:
thieves lick
shiny locks
pick futures
of grandchildren
to flush down
the pipelines that
fuel our maniac drives

driven to subtraction
we divide our longing
the glum in one another's arms
as manic waxes impressive
zips the slip to sex tax on fast cars
we glib subduction to crumple continents
humble condiments
a little relish to help out
a girl in a pickle

rides the convertible
            past limits
exchange rates be damned
            she
musters unaccountable
            pulls
a crash course
            in
revising derivatives
            from slum
to singing come-ons
            belt out
anthems of rebellion
            blow in and out
the city's stockades
            drowning or floating
she divides the clutch
            of authority's greed

fetishize the shift
   the lift-off of gentlemen
   it doesn't take a rocket scientist
     for a ride
       tanned hide remembers
       brutal skin
bruises   oozes
to flag our emblem
emperor disguised as little guy
   wins out
     against odds
and otter
   strange water mammal
     slicks into sea

post penetration,
                  broken water
fills the gap
           left behind
flaccid challengers
                  forgive the punctured body
oh christ!
          stigma traps chaotic depths
mannikin mouths
              the semblance of faith
but fetish, fiefdom, replicate
the money shot

                              obsession's seminal insistance
                    pulls capital
close as thieves   desire wired to the bomb
       the bomb that will keep us together
to pull the cycle closer
       nooses own neck
              don't ask me to plug the gap
       ask the gap to open
              diffuse
                     salt solution
              ocean we wash
       wide enough to hold
              that which floats and that which sinks

how i learned to strangelove my mom:
between captain and tenille,

                      a sunny cherish,
navigates empire's undertow,
as hollywood conquers and frankie runs screaming
into the arms of the stockbrokers,
nike breaststrokes leisurely: relax, just do it
let divas divest their
swansongs: *do you believe in life after love?*
throttle requires the empty space of the bottle,
but who ate the message?

genome dreams repetition compulsion
puppet meets jack
on a hook
stalks wither in contaminated field of vision
grasped the wrong vessel
message taps insistent
outside the box
junk manifests
our lobster rocks
bang bang
on the door

she drove a Plymouth satellite
faster than the speed of light
to the love hotel to the smack smack smack
of the catfish shack
all the while
knock knock knocking on chevron's door
pulling the master's strings
till she sets the night on fire
the oilfields are alive with the sound of mutiny

bounty's irate speech acts
"armed with chemical, biological and even
nuclear weapons"
incidental war hung in empty doorways
swing low sweet patriot
this is a sign of the crimes
we wring ghost hands
oh dear god
rhetoric reserved
no parking 24 h
violators will be ticketed and towed

coming for to carry me
to the land of social insecurity
missiles miss the point:
wealthy bombers can rot in hell
for all the righteous lies they tell
the camel's hump declares
the eye in the needle in the desert storm
stares in disbelief
at murderous republican conventions:
stars and pipes, oil and thiefdom
strangle us on the altar
as fundamentalists raise their fists, cry
four more years in self-fulfilling fervor
faster to armageddon

why do they worship the death of us all?

@merica

bell tolls in thrall
it rings for 'we'
our i's make a circle
bubble bursts speculation's sham
fall out heavy water
slavery's new master
flips binary
letter flops mopsy
boats swift their regloss
history's strategic remission
vets new lesions for legions
line our vietnam's ducks
rack arbitrary orients
to suit abuses
subject flourishes
a 'they' who can't see
by the dawn's early light

selling paradise
by the dashboard's might
hollywood glosses: let them drink coca-cola
while tanks rack up mileage
collapse the water table
crumble crumble oil and bumble
liars churn and exxon valdez tumbles
roadkill carcasses pile higher, mired, find
reboot won't do
as tons of sewage carry pesticides,
estrogen, prozac, pcbs into
the kitchen stinks

minx blinks
i think therefore i ham
laughter's carnivorous appetites
spills hunger greater than the sum
of all its larks
menagerie menages
circussing poll's substitutes
election's holy expletives
delete democracy's possibility
charisma calculated on collars per barrel
collossal collateral blings our boister
nuns sock noonday rockets
rage against the marine
this dirty wash
hung out to dry

ha ha ham
engineer a pig, blam
into the body of
a brown-skinned labourer, a synthetic sister
fill the laundromats, restaurants & factories with genetic menageries
secret squirrels, rambutanned rabbits, swollen salmon in st. john's
let class determine diet, choke on corporate canards
feeding the world license by license
one pat(i)ent at a time
ch-ch-ch-changes
only the cells can see

spare a dime
            the time
our pockets mint poppies
spasm nostalgia for wars
trenchant truncheons
policemen delineated front chivalry
surf capital's pretty coin
ride a dark horse to
molson canadian inscrutable mutates
projection hopping organisms
the silent nucleus hooded
suffers fluid injection
abu ghraib to secret lab
every byte's violin
ham strung to the last horse hair
the past drop

your pants &
wave the broken chemical lights:
the bible bellows
& the haliburton hell continues
walmart shoppers salute
then raise their fists
as the annals of national security
go anal:
bend over
& take it like a man, like it
or not, civilians are in
the panopticon eye and sweaty grasp
of the capitalist detention camp down south
even as we boycott
american tobacco, red meat & pharmaceutical industries
for replicating their republican stupidity
mammals and mamas mourn the banal coffins of progress
our grief slides into the veins, the lungs, the toenails
of dupont, del monte, philip morris, degrades
the dark coffers of freak trade

show and toll
autopsy reveals
       fascination addiction
       evidence forensic
victim's plush interior
this hour's décor
       irony of mourning
       doctor spins
rhetoric's archival record
to calculate heart rate's
       bloody valentine
       electronic coup marks
collective decimal
hexes parts per billion
       daily dosage doubles
       jeopardy
50s television shows
for 500

or 10,000 wishes, martyrs, hearts & fighter planes
exponents and square roots, proponents of rare suits,
the u.s. army gets ideas for weapons from mattel
& boys go marching one by one
a dying empire's hecatomb, as families cough up cash for
funerary corporations and stolen polls
those greedy christians want to own the afterlife
they'll leave mother earth behind but take us down with them

do you know the house of my abduction?
sieg heil of hades
basement of sick souls
birth of a nation
fallujah to my lai
"blood and flesh were spattered on the walls, witnesses said"
"it's certain that you can't bomb people into polling booths"
i ate the seeds
shot from severed limbs
our martin jayed
by rejigged meat puppet
countering cowboy to war president
further to fuhrer
expansive fear of righteous flock
the lord is my shepherd
i get what i want

I cry and I try and I cry and I try
I can't get no truce.
but don't get stuck in sad inaction
When I'm ridin' round the world
And I'm doin' this and I'm signin' that
for blood of your blood and flesh of my flesh
bless how burning visions press
in wartorn crèche
mammary lands
of milk and money

on the merry-go-round
        horses whore warehouse circuit
systematize repressed desire
clutch the candy-striped pole
love the spin you're in
        anything you want
        you've caught it
                our virus's linguistic twist
materializes the heavenly host
        in the war machine
scar chamber ridging evidence
slice until the cut won't heal anymore
        gnash the wound's dentata
a kiss is just a lisp
        languishing a dizzy bond

when lack of closure
triggers depression
what's a girl to do?
high risk investments
abound
          from TSE to BSE
the bull market
          surrounds
          her tender lips
its cycles of dust & doom
under the
dollar signed to the slyest bidder
          the unbearable heart
shakes and shudders
such a rift that
prayer falls ceaseless
the fearsome chasm
spasms
          vengeance
of the dispossessed
flash angry breasts
fossil fuels erotic offer
venous on the half shell

is manic to mantic
the leap from opium to snow?
read the flakes, crystals
take dirt, imperfections, to form
face precarious balaclavas
against weather &
the heart's flaws
futile or fugitive, might melt
with one strong beam

from miniscule origins
to mysterious ends
condensation nuclei
defy the odds
& even the temper's blows

tempest in a tea party
hatters rave ecstatic
mercury tips mescaline along weft of
soul's fabric, absorbs chemical effect
moral fibre seeks weave
and bob

a martial stance sublimated
to grace in motion
coup de coeur
or state of the union
not for the taint of heart

let others tell.
i am told out
s/he shot my perfect apple out
sundered me
my mouthy core
melts sound
down to the why, or tries
to make a chinese apple
into infinite pi
and you want to travel with heir
and you want to travel blind

decimal points in several directions
reason's cul de sac
the address of champions
we make our home in the air
pie in the sky
captain of my stark
raven my naked nest
snowing black feathers
the over of others
eggs me on

                    face it.
                    ain't over till
                                        the embryo shows
          the fetus sings
                    destiny prompts selenology:
                    chang o moans vows
                                        as the eggs'
          monthly release
                    reminds aerial letters'
                    recipients how
                                        blood comes
          earthly insistence
                    meteor or metaphor
                    it fortifies

universal recipient admits alphabet
        a's denial glances
b's pathology
the story of o: to give is not to take
        french kiss
standardized by e. u. regulations
        her all-accepting lack
antibodies this seismic shudder
        waves a shock of crust and mantle

b positive, wish the gift
        economy into b-ing
miss L and E, ooh la la
        c u cumming for
to carry me home
        in the anguish of language
slave to _ov_ or in or to or through
        predisposition from sanguine to the face
_ov_ music:
        redden my cheeks when the earth shakes
forth:
a socialist blush an anarchist bloom
        communal cravings don't subside
though capital incarcerates, distracts & distorts
the i-owe-you's have it: oui, vive l'amour

louis westernizes la revolucion
materializes conditions
for breakfast club
soft poached or over easy
prepositions deposit
movement silted in short vowels
readers digest instant message
smiley's icons plant worms
symbiotic systems feedback
labels loophole
this way out
the garden isn't gone
it was never there
utopia's ipod serenades regardless
want stands in for want
to whom it may concern

back in lack
  tilt the glass so that
    it's half full &
  hail the composting hero
    determined to cultivate her garden
    have hens lay gorgon eggs
  modus operandi:
    infiltrate as cells
    as model cidadans
      row house by row house
    median by meridian
    traffic in lavender,
    sage, edible weeds retake
  the city in which i lull you
out of consumerism
into loving the alien labour

o chicky
   dance if you want to
      leave your friends' hatchings
               grasshopper's aunt's all relative
      unzoned night hills throb insect talk
   mirror's defect plagues infection
       swarm from dull reverse
            liminal or vegetable?
collective forms sentient incident
     to sing is no trouble
         scrape leftovers to pattern
            maze of fresh detritus

the jobbly gene giant stomps out
      the maize
            thunders over gaia's song
but tantrum all he wants
     she's still larger than his life
   a scale of metonymy substitutes mineral for carnivore
babies' chickpea stomachs grow to walnuts then oranges
            sunkist & sunkicked
               from the cooperative's orchards
                  into the farmers' markets

grain elevates pooling peeps
collective hunger stills nomadic urge
    monsanto clause
    ruptured cell cooperates
        temp rising to new balance
        runner's stretch warrior one
            give lip or   slip   flip
            dirty bird on colonel's modified wing
            middle digitizes rhetoric's mediatized message
                    mutter ship
                calling for alien avian
                      to pidgin home

dirges burn on kernel's mogrified whim
muddle diligent returns, material missives
                              mauling crypts
                    crawling for agrarian liens
                              to piscines clone
                    ostrich preen or congee's sheen
          cells die for the greater ghoul –
                              it's antibio's trick
                    to treat us all, the shame

sham's enhancement entrances
real thing   coaxing the coats off our hacks
naked chefs saucing
modification to favour multiple unpredictable enchantments
apprentice's hubris floods mickey's drunken floor
dizzy master dons emperor's clothes
chance winces
accepts roll of die
verses' loss scripts wisdom of habitat
weather's thermometer swells meltwater   our floes current ice
gulfs wages ages   nurture forces froth
to tip the shale

a vowel disappears or disappoints, veers & bobs up & down:
                              i i i i i i i
balls get jiggled & juggled, fish off or flush luck
prongs, sproings, sprints towards the finish line:
                    multiple i's & multiple o's
          from classic to zero, dirty calories preserve the family joules
more polar bears drown as glaciers disappear, repeats back to u,
                    hand job or heart throb:
we're all blowing in the wind, fissile missives hit home:
               even lougheed calls a moratorium for what it is,
          nude bitumen to lewd crude will be the last big gasp
                    unless we learn to sage now

ego waffles   each indent engulfs its jam
        howl of the ow before o
ugh of the spew before u   a slick solution
        to dregs instead
personal is maniacal   wants breakfast at the pump
        lump sum consumption limited by seven sisters
avoiding flood of excess crude   accusing terror as tactic
to limit traffic on pipe lining silk road
        persia to china   the love that dare not speak its gain
    every environ atoms its national interest
                                gush to push fast on fascism
        while fumbling for a joy that sticks

it to the man: give eye teeth
or canine howl
for house of pomegranates
art in its own right & left, drapes a
long now
unfurls from seeds in the jelly
raspberry to rasputin
invoke a jammy whammy special
take a commodity vacation
as shares rise with desperate bids
gambling queens, dancing fiends
spin the mad machine
folie a deux, trois, quatre...
algorithm of the agon prism whirs

infinity ships fools
transit's madness trumps logic of cards
poker face slots cherry's choice
taxonomy redefines pluto's planetary status
if you don't play
you're still playing
king spades souls guarded by detention's club
or clover
crimson lie bathes
operatives' bloodlust
and diamonds dog child soldiers
hearts broken before they're grown
equation calculates even compassion
the rule of live and let cry

shuffle the tech
joker hoaxter pushes
rude buddhas & middle class barbarians
into the same soul train
sweatin' with the masses
on the metro race and gender clashes
ideals against crude awakenings
get off at the next stop
or keep riding in the hopes
of solar, wind, renewable courses
infinite transport & honest centres call
odds without ends

lama spams compassion
stance rations resist   to go with the flow
      is a slow slog   moxie boxed
about the ears   there's always a ringing
church bells ignite low swells of sad and had
sand and hand slipped a shucking knife
before oyster can muster
moon solidarity   here comes the tide
     too late to save slit muscle
grit and gristle adorning flayed flesh

thrash and pray? strapped and frayed
patients wait so disinfectant and needles do their work
hope for moxibustion herbs & smart deductions
but spit & spite prevail
upon the cloister as groundwater dries up
& red tide creeps, drops
the water table below space age couple's maverick muscles
what song could dispel fire and strafe, unholy waste?
plant your feet on this earth and flex your sandy toes to the sky
stay alert to remain handy
night trippy & day tricky

                    palmers cruise mother-of-pearl
long conquest precedes travel package's all-inclusive
                    jamaica and roma
my pall to your mall   your john to my con   no one escapes air
        nikes and psyches busted by the charm of karma
                              one-way ticket's vocation
                                        homeless returns
                    prison house of language materializes
for non-speakers   awake in the iron box
subaltern yowls against cat callers
          construction sites viral replication of creeks and counties
              enjoy the falsies
                              when the truth is too holey
                              for confidence men
                              hens lay eggs in the fox's den

dub elbows you, the world, into film reversions
throwback to blowback
head & breath through the heart
rejuice & reverberate
as you wait for kuwait
stay awake for the stakes
no monopoly & properly kissed
make it purr make it mew
make the bridge as you walk
back & forth, scratch & score
the page for more
murrelets, mycorrhizal mats
hail all blue wails
to walk strangers home

tree catches windfall
anxious spin wins unexpected gift
head bonked by the wonk of subterranean support
hat turns community chest
slopes hope through avenues mediterranean, baltic, oriental
incidental thimble dogs chance for tax rebate
on hotel construction
past go
every waterfront's memory of contact
hailed by jail
just visiting bereft
in the weft while warp goes on
stating ownership of web's reading railway
late of exception martyred & bartered
on security's earthly plane

red
suits
clowns and
criminals who aren't
papered in money's authority
venture capitalists park free forget
to thank fungal earth regenerating beneath asphalt
china creek disturbs the streets summons ancestral tunnels
immigration holds angel islands, handcuffs & bibles abound & go round
might missionaries harbour unexpected returns? some poisoned presents
can't be refused, just reused, exorcised, retooled for new
generations to instant message the future cell by cell
microbe by mycelia, vertebra by xylem
zygote by eukaryote, carapace
by axial stalk
critical mass
amends

pharmakon's carry-on contains accidental gel trips
reassuring ritual
clients' false comfort after uniform forces dumping of toothpaste
and hand cream
under the radar and
over the rainbow
coalition floats
nut too good to be true
karyotic mobility propelled
by cytoplasmic projections
all protections rejected by the animal within the animal
the mushroom in the restroom
spores mycorrhizal love across international airspace

a mammal kisses enamel
get down on your knees and spray
lotion in motion
enamoured of stranger and strangers
time-space travel from
urinals to Utah
ejaculates across the jetty
fill your empty thermos
with seeds for tomorrow
spiral dance or viral pranks
who can spill the difference?

hamburger today supersizes arable waste
        harbours staphylococcus, salmonella, e. coli and friends
   antibody becomes antigen
          immunoglobulin's internal rehearsal mirrors
                           external encounter
        déjà-vu   au-delà
   in democracy-to-come
        difference tests muddy water of same
                      seeks ion out of place
on the lightning field   metal rods tender quiver
           testing electrical air for second strike

an unlucky strike might lunge
                    into open pit mines, arsenic & cyanide tailings
dry fingers tap tap on keys that flushed nitrates into rivers
wet fingers pat raw meat into place, grilled & served with pickles
                    this little piggie in the mirror stages
                                        butchered ritual
mistakes the part for the hole in the earth
                    discarded computers get on a slow boat to china where
disemboweled circuit boards pile up, give gold bits &
                                        cancer to the villagers
                    can't drink the acid flowing along the shores?
            unpack cartons, suck poison from the sky
                    nicotine fits the addiction to devour
                    what's missing from this picture

                    the girl in the picture
                                                              not
missing exactly
                                        not there
              napalm naked
                        the one who speaks is not the girl in the
picture she is every fish the acid river coughs up every eater of
fish every arsenic atom pulsing or poisoning every breath you
take every piggy every burger hamming for the man every mush-
room every murrelet every mycorrhizal mat every lightning strike
                                        in the cameras of the world
            every every
and nothing but the lens's envy handing us our own hearts
    battered on platters
              shattered in stairwells
                              the girls know
                    they add what they know to what
                        they don't know what they feel
                                    to what they don't feel
                    what they have to what
                        they don't have what they are
                                    to what they are not
                                                        '
village in black smoke
      motherfather terror
                        running
              not the picture
              the thing
              not the thing
              the moment
              not the moment past
              the moment present
                    not the moment present
                              not not
                                        not never
              that

mercury & memory circulate faster as global tempo rises:

that
        dow sold napalm
                        bought union carbide

                        that dow
                        belongs to these icons:

                        bhopal baby girl face unburied
                        naked vietnamese girl
                                                running

bring that dow to market
                    to court
                            before thousands of unseen bodies
                            who lived in the earth

cu chi tunnels outran the invaders

                cavernous kitchens, dormitories, underground theatres

rice paddies & rubber trees grow back after the american war

                                        kiosks sprout
                                t-shirts and silent hurts
                what remains to be seen: redress

red dress swans brilliant feathers

                                                victor charlie
                    warps mutation to meet woof of return
confiscation refusal detainment
            slides democratic protest shakes author's corpse to life
        from dust to delight
wiggles truth's gleaming tooth
                        kernal precedes kinetic modification
    embedded love goddesses
miracle sapodilla, durian, lotus leaf, rambutan, eggfruit,
                                    custard apple
                                    swell from earth
rim before roll aches future content   enters breath
                floods atmosphere   buoys air
        silk unravels
        red redresses duress   undresses   recovers
                                    cell culture's defiant drag
        modifies mitochondria
joy ride to synthetic natural
                    parachute catches air to hold human aloft

122

Acknowledgements

As uninvited guests on the unceded traditional territories of the
Squamish, Musqueam and Tsleil Waututh peoples, we would like
to thank the Coast Salish peoples who remind us to respect the
land. The expression of such gratitude is not meant to smooth
over real conflicts due to violent land theft under colonization,
but to confirm our commitment to ally with the original cultures
of the land on which we live.

Sections of *sybil unrest* have been published as a chapbook by
Ashok Mathur, as well as in *West Coast Line, Open Letter,
The Golden Handcuffs Review, TCR (The Capilano Review),
XCP, The Windsor ReView* and *Prismatic Publics: Innovative
Canadian Women's Poetry and Poetics*.

This poem began in a renga spirit during the 2003 Hong Kong
International Literary Festival. It was a fraught moment — the
beginning of the SARS crisis in Hong Kong and the American
invasions of Iraq which we witnessed through the highly
interested sources of CNN and BBC on our hotel room TV.
Attending David Fujino and Aaron Vidaver's playful "july 23/03"
at the Kootenay School of Writing in Vancouver later that year
was the catalytic inspiration that actually got this poem off the
ground. *sybil unrest* is a back and forth conversation conducted
by email over the course of several months.

At our first public reading of the poem at the Kootenay School
of Writing on December 13, 2003, Fred Wah asked "Where
did the 'I' go?" "We" gesture towards how the personal sparks
this dialogue. "Ours" is not so much an individualized "I", but
rather a range of "i"s emerging and fading back as instances
that unsettle the (capitalist) time and space we occupy. As
such, the "i"s are not reliable but trace movement through the
long now and constitute evidence of some hopeful reaching
towards friendly coexistence of multiple tactics/perspectives.

The conversational format and the intensive questioning produce an unstable, flickering sort of subjectivity that throws an Enlightenment individual "I" into question, and hopefully exposes its ideological underpinnings. It is into this unstable subjectivity that we attempt to reinject questions of gender, race and class, as well as geography, movement, power and hope.

Phrases and rhythms, sometimes skewed, float in and out of *sybil unrest* from many places, including (in no particular order): jam. ismail (thank you for "iconomic"!), chuang tze, laurie anderson, cher, the b-52s, the rolling stones, leonard cohen, antonio machado, jane siberry, kd lang, led zeppelin, the situationists, tricky, massive attack, david bowie, judith butler, helene cixous, the book of ruth, bryan ferry, bob dylan, ac/dc, roy kiyooka, northrop frye, madonna, robert smithson, nick ut's photograph of phan thi kim phuc, various fairy tales, nursery rhymes, commercials, songs, films, and more. "The shock of recognition was overwhelming" comes from sharyn yuen's "Jook Kaak," a photography and handmade paper piece from 1990.

A few more references (acknowledged at widely varying levels of gratitude): colonel sanders, mr. christie, the bible, apple, fido, mcdonald's, trojan, air canada, singapore airlines, oscar and hammerstein, descartes, prince, blondie, shakespeare, american express, agatha christie, the smiths, frankie goes to hollywood, lewis carroll, john hughes, men without hats, jamie oliver, disney, lord alfred douglas, the beatles, gayatri spivak, arlen and harburg, jacques lacan, sting, dionne brand, tim horton's, ernest hemingway, u2, rage against the machine, maxwell house, michel foucault, giorgio agamben, jeopardy, roy orbison, herman hupfeld.

Big thank-yous to david fujino and aaron vidaver, ashok mathur, hiromi goto, roy miki, fred wah, david mckirdy, jam ismail, michael barnholden, ted byrne, walter k. lew, glen lowry, jacqueline turner, the kootenay school of writing, the hong kong international literary festival, and the canada council travel grants program.